AT THE STARTING LINE

PEOPLE PO

Kaitlyn Duling

Rourke

ROURKE'S
SCHOOL to HOME
CONNECTIONS

BEFORE AND DURING READING ACTIVITIES

Before Reading: *Building Background Knowledge and Vocabulary*

Building background knowledge can help children process new information and build upon what they already know. Before reading a book, it is important to tap into what children already know about the topic. This will help them develop their vocabulary and increase their reading comprehension.

Questions and Activities to Build Background Knowledge:

1. Look at the front cover of the book and read the title. What do you think this book will be about?
2. What do you already know about this topic?
3. Take a book walk and skim the pages. Look at the table of contents, photographs, captions, and bold words. Did these text features give you any information or predictions about what you will read in this book?

Vocabulary: *Vocabulary Is Key to Reading Comprehension*

Use the following directions to prompt a conversation about each word.

Read the vocabulary words.

- What comes to mind when you see each word?
- What do you think each word means?

Vocabulary Words:

- *agility*
- *endurance*
- *manikin*
- *navigate*
- *slalom*
- *triathlon*

During Reading: *Reading for Meaning and Understanding*

To achieve deep comprehension of a book, children are encouraged to use close reading strategies. During reading, it is important to have children stop and make connections. These connections result in deeper analysis and understanding of a book.

Close Reading a Text

During reading, have children stop and talk about the following:

- Any confusing parts
- Any unknown words
- Text to text, text to self, text to world connections
- The main idea in each chapter or heading

These strategies will help children learn to analyze the text more thoroughly as they read.

When you are finished reading this book, turn to the next-to-last page for **After-Reading Questions** and an **Activity**.

TABLE OF CONTENTS

READY TO RACE

Your heart is pounding. Your stomach is in knots. Your hands are sweaty. But the moment has come ... it's time to race!

People have been racing for thousands of years. Once they knew they could move fast ... they wanted to move *faster*!

Every single day, athletes across the globe line up to compete against others, against the clock, and against themselves.

Are you ready to race? Step up to the starting line and learn about the athletes who will run, swim, bike, climb, or whatever it takes to race to the finish.

ON THE RUN

Running is one of the oldest sports in human history. A footrace was held at the very first recorded Olympic Games in 776 BCE.

That race was called the stadion. Racers sprinted down the track, just like today's track stars. But they had to do it barefoot—and naked!

Today's Olympic sprinters are some of the fastest racers on foot. They race over short distances. In 2009, Jamaican sprinter Usain Bolt set the world record in the 100-meter sprint. He ran it in 9.58 seconds. That's about 23 miles per hour (37 kilometers per hour)! Bolt is known as the fastest man on the planet.

Sprint races are over in just a few seconds. **Endurance** athletes, on the other hand, like to go the distance! Endurance races come in a variety of distances and types.

The first modern Olympic games featured a marathon race. Today, marathon runners run 26.2 miles (42.2 kilometers). Some prefer a half-marathon: 13.1 miles (21.1 kilometers). For those who want an even greater challenge, there are ultra-marathons. Ultras can last hundreds or even thousands of miles.

endurance (en-DOOR-uhns): the ability to do something difficult for a long time

BARRIER-BREAKER

Kathrine Switzer was determined to run. In 1967, she became the first woman to officially register for and finish the Boston Marathon. Around mile 4, the race manager tried to pull her from the race—literally! But Switzer wouldn't back down. She just kept running. Today, nearly half of American marathon runners are women.

Runs come in all sorts of distances and themes. Some are held on roads. Others are run on trails. They can cover rolling hills or wind their way up mountains! There are races at night, in the morning, and even over 24 hours.

READY TO RUN?

Running isn't just for adults. Fun runs and 5k (5 kilometer) races are great ways for kids to get involved in running. Some schools and towns host their own youth running teams.

Many communities hold 5k races that are 3.1 miles long. Racers get into the spirit during holiday “turkey trots” and jingle bell runs. Some wear costumes or carry flags.

Running can make you hungry. Luckily, there are donut races. To finish, runners race a few miles, eat a dozen donuts, and then race more miles. Does it taste good? Probably. Does it feel good? That’s another story!

Wheelchair racers compete too! They speed down the road in specially built racing chairs.

SWIMMING AND CYCLING

Running isn't the only way to race. A **triathlon** combines three different sports. First, athletes go for a swim. Then, they mount their bikes. Finally, they lace up their running shoes!

triathlon (triye-ATH-lahn): a long-distance race made up of three parts that usually include swimming, bicycling, and running

The swimming leg of a triathlon is tough. Swimming uses almost all of an athlete's muscle groups. There are numerous ways swimmers can compete. After the first indoor swimming pool opened in 1828, swimmers began racing in pools to see who could swim the fastest!

SPLASH!

In swimming races, athletes must use certain styles, called strokes. Four of the main strokes are:

- **Backstroke**
- **Butterfly**
- **Breaststroke**
- **Freestyle**

Swimmers who love nature can try open water swims. In these races, swimmers conquer lakes, rivers, seas, and even oceans.

Open-water swims don't have any lane markings. Swimmers just dive in and swim hard toward the finish line. They battle against waves, wind, and weather. They might even spot some sea creatures!

ON THE WATER

Some water races take place on top of the water. Canoe sprints challenge athletes to paddle canoes or kayaks. Rowing, or crew, is one of the oldest Olympic sports. Crew races are called "regattas."

Surf lifesaving is a unique and practical set of races. Popular across New Zealand and Australia, the races combine multiple lifesaving activities.

These races include open-water swims, beach races, and more. Athletes even compete to rescue **manikins** from the water. These skills may help athletes land a lifeguard job!

manikins (MAN-i-kinz): models of the human body used for medical training

When it comes to cycle sports, racers have almost endless options. They can bike around a track, through dirt courses, or on grass. The most extreme cyclists compete in cycling endurance races like the Tour de France.

The Tour de France is known as the most important, the largest, and the most difficult bike race on Earth. Established in 1903, this race lasts more than 20 days and covers thousands of miles.

During the race, cyclists climb across five mountain ranges. They may be sweaty and sore, and some may even fall or crash. Supportive fans line the entire route. They hold signs, cheer, and celebrate this national French sporting event.

FINDING THEIR WAY

Many races use a track or course. Others are point-to-point. They might go from one city to another, or even one country to another.

Some brave racers have taken up a new challenge: orienteering. In an orienteering race, there is no set course. Racers use a map, compass, or radio to **navigate**. No cell phones allowed!

An extreme form of orienteering is called adventure racing. These races can take weeks and cover hundreds of miles. Teams complete several sections as quickly as possible. They may need to run, climb, bike, or paddle to the finish line.

navigate (NAV-i-gate): to find where you are and where you need to go

Sometimes, to win a race, you've got to freeze first! Some of the most popular racing sports are done in cold weather.

Speed skaters race around an oval track. They have to be fast—and careful. Sharp skates slice across the ice, close to their bodies. To stay safe, speed skaters wear thick gloves and protective "skin" suits.

While skaters go 'round and 'round the track, other athletes race down mountains! Snowboard and ski racing are popular winter sports.

Some of the races go straight down a hill. Others are **slalom** style. In slalom, racers must swerve between poles or gates. For cold-weather racers, there's no cooler feeling than skiing through the finish line!

slalom (SLAH-luhm): a sporting event in which competitors ski or snowboard down a hill, zigzagging between poles

One downhill race in Gloucester, England, is more of a chase. During the Cooper's Hill Cheese Roll, athletes chase a wheel of cheese down a 600-foot (200-yard) hill. Whoever catches the wheel first, wins. Their prize? The wheel of cheese, of course!

PERSON VS. HORSE

Sure, competing against other people is fun. But could you outrun a horse? Each year, participants in the "Man vs. Horse" race do just that. Horses usually win! Only three humans have triumphed since the race was first run in Wales in 1980.

Maybe you prefer to run up rather than down. For that, there's the Empire State Building Run Up. During this tower race, athletes tackle 86 flights. That's 1,576 stairs! The fastest runners can reach the top in about 10 minutes. If that sounds too tiring, there's always the elevator: It reaches the top in under a minute.

OVERCOMING OBSTACLES

Obstacle course races challenge athletes to climb, crawl, swing, jump, and run their way to the finish. The races test speed and **agility**. Some of the first obstacle races were run in military training. Today, obstacle gyms around the world train athletes to compete in local races and even on television.

Obstacle course races can get messy—really messy. Athletes may be asked to crawl through mud or climb monkey bars over water. From fire pits to slippery stairs, obstacle courses take racing to the next level.

agility (uh-JIL-i-tee): the ability to move fast and quickly

Time to climb! In 2020, sport climbing officially became an Olympic event. The event has three parts:

In lead climbing, athletes race to see how high they can climb.

In bouldering, athletes use their strength to pull themselves up huge boulders.

In speed climbing, athletes compete to see who can reach the top first.

Speed climbers race side-by-side. After the starting beep, the climbers zoom up the wall. They grip holds along the way. At the top, a button stops the clock. Speed climbs are *really* speedy. They can last just a few seconds!

For almost as long as humans have lived on Earth, they have been racing. Different places are known for different races. In China, racing on stilts is popular. In Egypt, there are sandboard races. In Namibia, sand-skiing!

There are countless ways to race—and races to be won all over the world. Win or lose, there's nothing quite like the feeling of crossing the finish line!

MEMORY GAME

Look at the pictures. What do you remember reading on the pages where each image appeared?

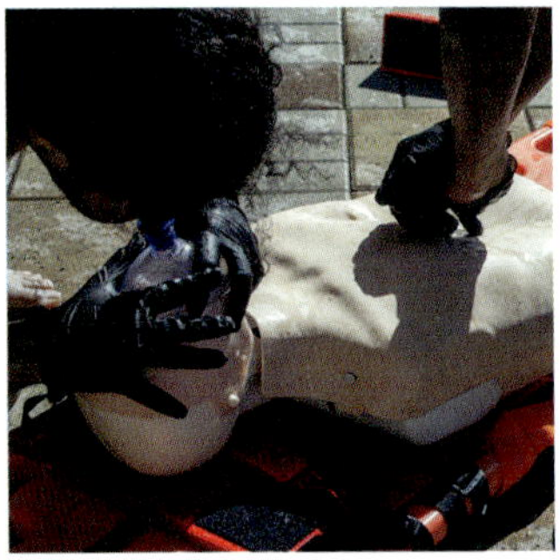

INDEX

AFTER-READING QUESTIONS

1. Why do you think people enjoy competing in races?
2. What are three different types of people-powered races?
3. How are sprint and endurance races different?
4. Why would a racer need navigation skills?
5. What are some ways in which you could get involved in racing?

ACTIVITY

Theme races—from the Santa Shuffle to the Donut Dash—inspire people of all ages to move their bodies. Think about a theme race you'd like to run or walk. Write out the rules of your race and plan the route. Then, invite friends or family members to run it with you. Remember, costumes make any race more fun!

ABOUT THE AUTHOR

Kaitlyn Duling is an avid runner. She's completed four marathons and countless races. She loves to sprint across the finish line with her wife, Hannah, by her side. When she's not running, Kaitlyn is writing in Boston, Massachusetts. (No, she hasn't run the Boston Marathon—yet!) She has authored more than 100 books for kids and teens.

www.rourkebooks.com

PHOTO CREDITS: cover, title page: ©Anton Vierietin/ Getty Images, ©Iurii Osadchi/ Shutterstock.com, ©Eduard Moldoveanu/ Shutterstock.com, ©FocusDzign/ Shutterstock.com; title page, pages 4-7, 12-13, 18-19, 24-25, 30-32: ©zoulgraph/ Shutterstock.com, page 4: ©Dejan Novakov/ Shutterstock.com; page 5: ©NizamD/ Shutterstock.com, ©junrong/ Shutterstock.com, ©Paolo Bona/ Shutterstock.com; page 6: ©Nastasic/ Getty Images, ©patrickds/ Getty Images, ©Historica Graphica Collection / Heritage Images/Newscom; page 7: ©patrickds/ Getty Images, ©Salty View/ Shutterstock.com; page 8: ©Joseph Sohm/ Shutterstock.com, ©Stable Air Media/ Shutterstock.com; page 9: ©Stable Air Media/ Shutterstock.com, ©Chema Moya/EFE/Newscom, ©Joseph Sohm/ Shutterstock.com; page 10: ©Jana Herzberg/ Shutterstock.com; page 11: ©Sunshine Seeds/ Shutterstock.com, ©Chris Mole/ Shutterstock.com, ©Thongden Studio/ Shutterstock.com; page 12: ©Pavel1964/ Shutterstock.com, ©NizamD/ Shutterstock.com, ©EvrenKalinbacak/ Shutterstock.com; page 13: ©Brycia James/ Getty Images, ©Gert Vrey/ Shutterstock.com; page 14: ©Kirillm/ Getty Images, ©John Kropewnicki/ Shutterstock.com; page 15: ©PomInOz/ Shutterstock.com, ©PlataRoncallo/ Shutterstock.com; page 16: ©Karen I. Hirsch/ZUMA PRESS/Newscom; page 17: ©Radu Razvan/ Shutterstock.com; page 18: ©Juriah Mosin/ Shutterstock.com; page 19: ©Juriah Mosin/ Shutterstock.com, ©Mikhail Pankov/ Shutterstock.com; page 20: ©Michele Morrone/ Shutterstock.com, ©schankz/ Shutterstock.com; page 21: ©schankz/ Shutterstock.com, ©Maxim Petrichuk/ Shutterstock.com, ©action sports/ Shutterstock.com; page 22: ©Mirrorpix/Newscom; page 23: ©Aled Llywelyn/ZUMA PRESS/Newscom, ©secheve8/ Shutterstock.com, ©lev radin/ Shutterstock.com; page 24: ©ya_create/ Shutterstock.com; page 25: ©Mike Stotts/Splash News/Newscom, ©Blulz60/ Shutterstock.com, ©Robert Perry/ZUMA Press/Newscom; page 26: ©SolStock/ Getty Images, ©Angelika Warmuth/dpa/picture-alliance/ Newscom, ©cbradder/ Shutterstock.com; page 27: ©Jasmin Walter/ZUMA PRESS/Newscom; page 28: ©imageBROKER/Fabian von Poser/Newscom; page 28: ©Sun_Shine/ Shutterstock.com, ©TPG/ZUMA Press/Newscom; page 29: ©Anastasios71/ Shutterstock.com, ©Daniel A. Anderson/ZUMA PRESS/Newscom; page 30: ©Mirrorpix/Newscom, ©Mikhail Pankov/ Shutterstock.com, ©PlataRoncallo/ Shutterstock.com, ©Brycia James/ Getty Images, ©Chris Mole/ Shutterstock.com, ©Historica Graphica Collection / Heritage Images/Newscom

Edited by: Laura Malay
Cover design by: Alison Tracey
Interior design by: Alison Tracey

Library of Congress PCN Data

People Power / Kaitlyn Duling
(At the Starting Line)
ISBN 978-1-73165-734-3 (hardcover)
ISBN 978-1-73165-721-3 (softcover)
ISBN 978-1-73165-747-3 (e-book)
ISBN 978-1-73165-760-2 (e-pub)
Library of Congress Control Number: 2023933036

Rourke Educational Media
Printed in the United States of America
02-3042411937